Just Being One

Ray Andrews

For you,

and all friends of truth everywhere.

My special thanks to

Rachna Chowla (poet) and Anna Fraser (illustrator)

for their invaluable expertise and creative help.

If you pass this way

Put your burden down

Pour tea

And drink slowly

Walking on a sandy beach

Footprints follow

When I stop

They catch up

The rose petal

Speaks many languages

It's a wonder

We understand

The desert gate

Is lock-less

Fence-less

And has a squeaky hinge

Fortunately

Love is a mystery

Otherwise

We would never fall

The mountain

Waits patiently

For climbers

To change their views

The wonder of nature

Is that it constantly

Ignores

Me

When we meet again

Let it be Springtime

Our thoughts and feelings

Will be compost by then

When the ripples subsided

The fish had disappeared

Memory floated a while

Then sank

Smiling to the echo

Reminded me

To watch out

For boomerangs

I've been finding treasure

Everywhere lately

Now I know

Who buried it

A silver thread

Is woven into life's tapestry

For children

To unravel

There is no need

To simplify

That's far too complicated

Before the sun rises

There is waiting

Longing

Then the blinding light

In the lake

The heron's beating wings

Are mirrored

In stillness

Leaving the downy nest

Far behind

The fledged birds

Become sky and distant mountains

A raindrop

Entered a circular doorway

And instantly became

A woodland lake

It's difficult

To be serious

When a small bird

Sings and flies

You have to be completely lost

So as to discover

That no one left

In the first place

The first time we met

I fell in love

Now every time we meet

Nothing changes

The tortoise

Has no need to hurry

She is home

All the time

Yesterday

You spoke to me

Today

I am listening

Last night

My bedroom got flooded in moonlight

I thought to close the curtains

But drowned happily instead

The meadow is overflowing

In birdsong

Making my skylark

Restless

Sitting beside the tent

Eating breakfast

Tasting

The peace

Sometimes our hearts

Grow so much

They cease caring

Who the owner is

When we are born

So too is death

And when we die

So too does death

A tear

Fell slowly

In an ocean

Of joy

God

Cannot give us anything

He has given us everything

Already

When I look carefully

There is only you

Dressed in your coat

Of many colours

We are reeds

Whispering

We are shadows

Flowing to the sea

There is nothing

But nothing

But nothing

As white as blossom

On a sunny day

Waves break

On the shoreline of ourselves

Sighing with relief

In the sand

Birdsong

Is the woodland spring

Inside

You

Wake up

And enjoy life's porridge

Being stirred

In the morning sun

Of all the wonders in life

A child's simple gaze

Can easily

Hold them all

Oh! what joy breathing

A hedgerow

Tangled

With fragrant honeysuckle

As the rose bud

Unfurls

The roots

Curl their toes

On the empty beach

I looked into my lover's eyes

Only to find myself

Smiling

There are love messages
Written in the sand
That even the tide
Refuses to delete

Regardless of the cost

To smile at one's own reflection

Is not asking

So very much

As the bus driver reversed

The passengers

Did not know

Whether they were coming or going

The problem is

There is no problem

And therefore

No solution

Now the river spoke

And I watched myself

In wonder

Floating by

For the mountain stream

To make its journey

The snow must melt

And leave its colour behind

Sky

And lake

Make

Perfect lovers

Your flesh

Talking to my skin

Listening to your eyes

Touching my mouth

Behind the cloud

The moon floats

Bathing

In sunshine

During the night
A fox walked on the lake
And left a footprint
In my frozen heart

The geese are leaving

They travel light

No baggage

No passport

No sky

Flower petals
Fall at midnight
While bees
Lie sleeping

Is it really you moon

In the birdbath

Filling my eyes

With moonshine?

The jackdaws' harsh cries

In the bell tower

Never change

Whether a wedding or funeral

On the soldier's grave

A blackbird sings

A primrose grows

Beside a wooden bench
In the churchyard
A daisy slept peacefully
In the moonlight

Mary

Stood watching

While the church mice played

On the stained glass floor

During the summer storm

The deserted deck chairs

Enjoy

The sea view

I gave my love

A wild rose

But did not realise

My heart would be the vase

My door is always open

To let the stars in

It's wide enough for a herd of elephants

So please do come in

The pearl

Is never hidden

From

Itself

Remember

When you face the light

Your shadow

Takes a steady look at you

Without me

Life is unthinkable

So

I am always here

Over the stream

A heron's shadow passed

Sending a ripple

Through my heart

Who is there

In my eyes?

Tears

Cannot wash you away

Love

Whispered to me

Now I lie awake

And cannot sleep

Precious little

Remains

On the pathway

To the sun

Darkness
Lights the stars
Then disappears
In their light

Each day
My castle
Changes back
To sand